VIENNA

teNeues

VIENNA

Photographs by Tina and Horst Herzig
Text by Dodo Kresse

teNeues

Sprechen Sie es aus, dieses Wort „Wien" und schon zieht sich das lange „i" sehnsüchtig wie das Biegen einer brokatumhüllten Taille im Walzertakt. Die Melodien von Strauß und Schubert haben sich so innig mit den verwinkelten Gassen und Häusern der Innenstadt verbunden, dass der zarte Nachhall immer noch in der Luft liegt. Besonders in der Früh, wenn die Sonne die Kuppel der Hofburg beleuchtet und die goldene Blätter-Kugel der Secession zum Glänzen bringt, zeigt sich Wien poetisch und von zauberhaftem Wesen. Dann versteht man die Vermutung, Wien sei auf einem Notenblatt entstanden. Zart, melancholisch und selbstbewusst. Die 4,4 Kilometer lange Ringstraße umfasst den Edelstein „Innenstadt" mit duftenden Kastanien-Alleen. Jedes Haus atmet Geschichte. Während einer Tour rund um den Ring inhaliert man mehr Architektur-Know-how als dies ein Lehrbuch vermitteln könnte. Nehmen Sie die Kutsche – in Wien „Fiaker" genannt. Rathaus, Parlament, Hofburg, Burgtheater, Oper – jedes Bauwerk wurde in einem anderen Stil entworfen und dennoch ergänzt das eine das nächste. Jugendstil-Fetischisten genießen das Fassaden-Schauen im Naschmarkt-Bereich, der Gotik-Freund bestaunt den Stephansdom, dessen Bausubstanz durch das viele Renovieren tatsächlich nur mehr zu 30 Prozent aus der Gotik stammt. Barocke Gemüter spazieren zur Karlskirche und jene mit mystischem Hang lassen sich von der ältesten Kirche der Stadt, der Ruprechtskirche im Judenviertel inspirieren. Im Kern der Stadt flaniert man am Kohlmarkt, am Graben und auf der Kärntner Straße. Autos haben hier nichts verloren, die Straßen gehören den einkaufslustigen Nasen-an-den-Scheiben-platt-Drückern, den mondänen Ladies, die bei Chanel, Gucci und Sander „reinschauen", den flippigen Teenagern, die ihr Geld bei H&M und Pimkies in trendiges Outfit verwandeln. Dazwischen pausiert man in den Wiener Kaffeehäusern. Fern von jeder verkitschten Bemühung um eine glitzernde Vergangenheit, sind diese so authentisch, dass der Blueberry-Muffin aus dem Coffee-Shop daneben zwar seine Daseinsberechtigung hat, aber das ist dann auch schon alles. Ein richtiger Guglhupf ist eben doch was „ganz anderes". Frisch gestärkt geht's abends entweder auf die Donau-Insel, wo getanzt und gelacht wird. Ob fetziges Roller-Skaten oder genüssliche Mondschein-Bootsfahrten – die Insel holt jeden ins Entertainment-Paradies. Oder man fährt hinaus zu den Heurigen nach Grinzing und gönnt sich jungen Wein und ein „Bratlfett'n-Brot", das trotz Internationalisierung der Speisekarte eisern seinen Platz verteidigt.

Inmitten der „grantelnden" Wiener Gesellschaft wächst eine Generation heran, die sich das „Raunzen" aus den Adern gewaschen hat. Denn darin fließt höchst heiteres Blut. Man ist modern, erfreut sich an Innovation und liebt Fremdländisches. Wien ist ein Schmelztiegel geworden, der das Unbekümmerte der Italiener, das Avantgardistische der Londoner, das Hedonistische der Pariser und das Effiziente der New Yorker zu einer einmaligen Melange vermischt. Eine überschaubare Welt-Metropole hat sich zu Recht einen der vordersten Ränge in puncto Lebensqualität und Kultur errungen.

Dodo Kresse

Say the word "Vienna" and the sound of the "i" rings out, just as longingly as the movement of a figure in a finely brocaded ballgown, dancing to the rhythm of a waltz. The melodies of Strauß and Schubert are so intimately connected with winding backstreets and buildings in downtown Vienna that the gentle strains of music are still in the air. Early morning, especially when the sun lights up the dome of the Hofburg and the golden leaves sparkle on the spherical roof of Vienna's Secession, the city shows off its poetic and magical charm. It is easy to see why suspicions were awakened that Vienna was created on a music score. Delicate, melancholy and self-confident. Vienna's main street, the Ringstraße, a circuit of 4.4 km running round the jewel of the city, is flanked by avenues of chestnut trees and filled with the scent of their sweet aroma. Each building has an air of history. Take a tour around the "Ring" and you can breathe more architectural know-how than any textbook can teach. Try a ride in a horse and carriage—the Viennese call it "Fiaker". Vienna's town hall, parliament, Hofburg, Burgtheater, Opera House—every building is designed in a different style and, still, one thing complements the next. Anyone with a fetish for *Jugendstil* will enjoy looking at this architectural style on the façades in the Naschmarkt district. For the lover of Gothic, St. Stephen's cathedral is a treat, even if endless renovations mean only about 30% of the building is actually original Gothic. Fans of baroque should take a walk to the St. Charles Church and anyone with a head for the mystical must make for the city's oldest church of St. Ruprecht, an inspirational place in the Jewish Quarter. In downtown Vienna, you can wander about the Kohlmarkt, the Graben, and on the main street, Kärntner Straße, the cars have not even lost out: the streets belong to shoppers who press their noses right up against the windows; chic ladies "just looking" at Chanel, Gucci and Sander, or the way-out teenager, turning money into trendy outfits, like at H&M and Pimkies. Any number of Viennese coffee houses are good for a break. The coffee house is authentic Vienna; no sign of kitsch and recreating a glitzy past here. The blueberry muffin in the coffee shop next door has nothing more than a right to exists—a real "Guglhupf" (a speciality pastry) is "something else". All refreshed and ready for the nightlife? Try either the Danube-island for dancing and amusements, from crazy roller skating, or pleasure cruises by moonlight—the island beckons every visitor to enjoy an entertainment paradise. Or else, take a ride out to a wine cellar, the "Heurigen" at Grinzing, and treat yourself to new wine and a "Bratlfett'n-Brot", a speciality which resolutely keeps its place on the menu, despite the international selection.

Amidst a "complaining" Viennese society, a new generation is growing up, without the "moodiness" running through its veins, because lively spirits flow here. In Vienna, they are modern, they delight in innovation and love anything from afar. The city has grown into a melting pot, where carefree Italians, avantgarde Londoners, hedonist Parisians and efficient New Yorkers mingle in a unique blend. An international metropolis that is easy to get around has earned its just reward, climbing to the top rank for quality of lifestyle and culture.

Dodo Kresse

Prononcer le mot « Vienne » et le « i » s'élance et glisse comme une danseuse au rythme d'une valse. Les musiques de Strauß et de Schubert imprègnent si profondément la ville qu'elles résonnent encore dans les ruelles et les maisons. Surtout tôt le matin, quand le soleil illumine la coupole de la Hofburg et fait briller les feuilles dorées de la Sécession, la poésie et la magie de Vienne apparaissent dans toute leur splendeur. Dans ce cadre, il n'est pas difficile de s'imaginer que Vienne a été créée sur une page de musique : douce, mélancolique et sûre d'elle. La Innenstadt, telle une pierre précieuse, est sertie dans un feuillage de marronniers odorants qui jalonnent la Ringstraße, longue de 4,4 kilomètres. Chaque maison respire l'histoire. En se promenant sur le Ring, l'on apprend plus sur l'architecture que dans n'importe quel livre. Prenez le fiacre et découvrez la ville! L'hôtel de ville, le parlement, la Hofburg, le Burgtheater, l'Opéra, chaque édifice a un style différent mais tous se complètent de manière harmonieuse. Les spécialistes de *Jugendstil* admireront les façades du Naschmarkt, le Stephansdom enchantera l'amateur de style gothique même si 30 pour cent seulement de l'édifice sont d'époque, à cause des rénovations successives. Les visiteurs attirés par le baroque apprécieront la Karlskirche, les mystiques seront inspirés par la Ruprechtskirche, l'église la plus ancienne de la ville située dans le quartier juif. Le cœur de la ville, le Kohlmarkt, le Graben et la Kärntner Straße appartiennent aux flâneurs et non aux voitures : les promeneurs peuvent faire du lèche-vitrine, les élégantes passer chez Chanel, Gucci et Sander, et la jeunesse branchée échanger son argent contre des tenues à la mode chez H&M et Pimkies. Entre deux achats, on fait une pause dans un café viennois. Loin de toute imitation kitsch du passé, ces cafés sont si authentiques que les muffins aux myrtilles du coffee-shop d'à côté, aussi bons soient-ils, ne peuvent pas rivaliser avec un vrai « Guglhupf ». Après s'être requinqué, la visite continue le soir sur l'île du Danube où l'on se retrouve pour danser et s'amuser. Que ce soient les courses de rollers ou les promenades en bateau au clair de lune, l'île est un paradis de divertissements où tout le monde trouve son bonheur. On peut aussi se rendre à Grinzing pour déguster dans les « Heurigen » (tavernes) le vin nouveau avec un « Bratlfett'n-Brot », une spécialité très prisée, malgré une cuisine de plus en plus internationale.

Les vieux Viennois sont connus pour être ronchons mais ce n'est plus le cas de la génération montante. Le Viennois d'aujourd'hui est moderne, ouvert à l'innovation et à la différence. Vienne est devenue un melting-pot dont est issue une nouvelle société que caractérisent l'insouciance de l'Italien, l'esprit d'avant-garde du Londonien, la mentalité hédoniste du Parisien et l'efficacité du New-Yorkais. Vienne est une métropole aux dimensions humaines qui compte aujourd'hui à juste titre parmi les villes avec une qualité de vie et une offre culturelle exceptionnelles.

Dodo Kresse

Pronuncie esta palabra, "Viena", y la "i" ya se estira anhelante como el giro de una cintura envuelta en brocado al compás del vals. Las melodías de Strauß y Schubert se han unido tan profundamente a las callejuelas llenas de rincones y las casas del centro de la ciudad que el suave eco todavía está en el aire. Especialmente por la mañana, cuando el sol alumbra la cúpula del Hofburg y da brillo a las doradas bolas en forma de hojas de la Secesión, Viena se muestra poética y con una esencia mágica. Entonces uno comprende la suposición de que Viena ha surgido de una partitura. Suave, melancólica y segura de sí misma. La Ringstraße, de 4,4 kilómetros de longitud, abarca la joya del "Centro Urbano" con avenidas de olorosos castaños. Todas las casas respiran historia. Durante una vuelta por el Ring se inhalan más conocimientos de arquitectura de los que podría trasmitir un libro. Tome un coche de caballos, llamado en Viena Fiaker. El Ayuntamiento, el Parlamento, el Hofburg, el Burgtheater, la Ópera, cada edificio se proyectó en un estilo diferente y, sin embargo, cada uno complementa al otro. Los fetichistas del modernismo disfrutan mirando las fachadas en la zona del Naschmarkt, los amigos del gótico contemplan la Stephansdom cuya estructura, debido a las muchas reformas, ya sólo procede realmente del gótico en un 30 por ciento. Ánimos barrocos pasean hacia la Karlskirche y aquellos con tendencia mística se dejan inspirar por la iglesia más antigua de la ciudad, la Ruprechtskirche en el Barrio Judío. En el centro de la ciudad uno callejea por el Kohlmarkt, el Graben y por la Kärntner Straße. Aquí los automóviles no han perdido nada, las calles pertenecen a los compradores que pegan la nariz contra los escaparates, a las señoras elegantes que entran en Chanel, Gucci y Sander, a los adolescentes desenfadados que transforman su dinero en looks de moda en H&M y Pimkies. Entre una cosa y otra, se hace una pausa en los cafés vieneses. Lejos de todo esfuerzo cursi por un pasado brillante, estos cafés son tan auténticos que, a su lado, el Blueberry-Muffin del Coffee-Shop tiene su razón de ser pero eso es todo. Es que un pastel de molde (Guglhupf) de verdad es "algo totalmente diferente". Recién fortalecido, uno se va por las noches a la isla del Danubio, donde se baila y se rie: Patinadores marchosos o deliciosos viajes en barco a la luz de la luna, la isla transporta a cada uno al paraíso de la animación. O se marcha a los "Heurigen" de Grinzing para concederse un vino joven y una especialidad del lugar (Bratlfett'n-Brot) que, a pesar de la internacionalización del menú, defiende su puesto férreamente.

En medio de la "refunfuñona" sociedad vienesa crece una generación que se ha lavado esa actitud de sus venas. Pues en ellas fluye, como mucho, sangre alegre. La gente es moderna, se alegra ante las innovaciones y ama lo exótico. Viena se ha convertido en un crisol que, en una mezcla excepcional, combina lo despreocupado de los italianos, lo vanguardista de los londinenses, lo hedonista de los parisinos y lo eficiente de los neoyorquinos. Una metrópoli mundial abarcable ha conquistado con derecho uno de los puestos delanteros en lo que respecta a calidad de vida y cultura.

Dodo Kresse

Dite Vienna, anzi no, "Wien", che con questa lunga "i" risveglia la nostalgia, come fianchi avvolti in broccato che ondeggiano a tempo di valzer. Le melodie di Strauß e di Schubert si sono unite così strettamente alle viuzze tortuose e alle case del centro storico, che l'eco soave risuona ancora nell'aria. Il mattino specialmente, quando il sole illumina la cupola dell'Hofburg e fa scintillare la sfera di foglie dorate della Secessione, Vienna appare nel suo carattere poetico e incantevole. Allora si capisce perché si dice che Vienna sia nata su un pentagramma. Soave, malinconica e sicura di sé. Il Ring, circonvallazione di 4400 metri, con i suoi viali odorosi di castagni, racchiude il cuore della città come una gemma. Ogni casa è pregna di storia. In un giro per il Ring si respirano più nozioni di architettura di quante ne possa trasmettere un libro specializzato. Prendete la carrozza o, per meglio dire, il fiacre. Rathaus, Parlamento, Hofburg, Burgtheater, Opera – ogni edificio è stato progettato in uno stile diverso, tuttavia l'uno completa l'altro. I fanatici dello *Jugendstil* si godono le facciate sul Naschmarkt, gli amanti del gotico ammirano il duomo di Santo Stefano, i cui materiali da costruzione, a causa dei ripetuti restauri, risalgono al gotico per poco più del trenta per cento. Chi per indole inclina al barocco si fa una passeggiata fino alla Karlskirche e chi ha una vena mistica si lascia ispirare dalla chiesa più antica della città, la Ruprechtskirche, nel quartiere ebraico. Nel centro della città si va a spasso per il Kohlmarkt, al Graben e per la Kärntner Straße. Qui le auto non sono ammesse, le strade appartengono a chi fa shopping con il naso appiccicato alle vetrine, alle signore eleganti che "fanno un salto" da Chanel, Gucci e Sander, agli adolescenti un po' strambi, che all'H&M e al Pimkies trasformano il loro denaro in un look trendy. Ogni tanto una pausa nei caffè viennesi. Lontani da ogni riproduzione commerciale di un passato radioso, i caffè sono così autentici che i muffin al mirtillo del coffee-shop accanto hanno sì il diritto di esistere, ma solo quello. Un vero "Guglhupf" all'uvetta è proprio un'altra cosa! Rifocillati, la sera si può andare sull'isola del Danubio, dove si ride e si balla. Ci si lanci sui pattini o ci si abbandoni al piacere di una gita in barca al chiaro di luna: l'isola trascina tutti nel paradiso del divertimento. Oppure si può andare un po' fuori negli "Heurige", i locali tipici di Grinzing a godersi il vino novello con il "Bratlfett'n-Brot", piatto che difende saldamente la sua posizione a dispetto di un menù ormai internazionale.

Nel mezzo della società viennese brontolona sta crescendo una generazione che si è scrollata di dosso il malumore. La serenità sta entrando nel sangue. Si è moderni, innovativi e xenofili. Vienna è diventata un crogiolo in cui si fondono in una miscela unica la noncuranza degli italiani, l'avanguardia dei londinesi, l'edonismo dei parigini e l'efficienza dei newyorkesi. Una piccola metropoli internazionale ha ottenuto a buon diritto uno dei primi posti per qualità della vita e cultura.

Dodo Kresse

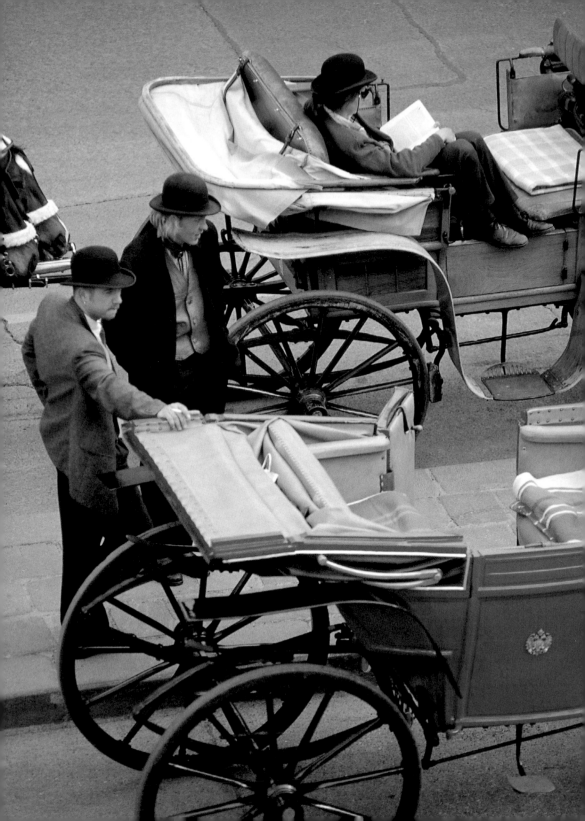

19., Grinzinger Allee

Wieselburger Bier seit 1770

Grinzinger
Käsespätzle mit
grünem Salat 5,80

Rahmbeuschel
mit Knödel 6,20

Wieselburger Bier seit 1770

Welsfilet in
Bärlauchbutter
gebraten, dazu
Tagliolini 11

Gebackener
Camembert
mit Preiselbeere

Verzeichnis Directory Table des matières Directorio Indice delle materie

Front cover: Neue Hofburg
Back cover: Café Sperl, Gumpendorfer Straße

Photographs © 2003 Tina and Horst Herzig
© 2003 teNeues Verlag GmbH + Co. KG, Kempen
All rights reserved.

www.herzig-foto.de

Picture and text rights reserved for all countries.
No part of this publication may be reproduced in
any manner whatsoever. All rights reserved.

Photographs by Tina and Horst Herzig
Design by Anika Leppkes, teNeues Verlag
Introduction by Dodo Kresse
Translation by SWB Communications,
Dr. Sabine Werner-Birkenbach, Mainz
Dr. Suzanne Kirkbright (English)
Dominique Le Pluart (French)
Gemma Correa-Buján (Spanish)
Evita Santopietro (Italian)
Editorial coordination by Kristina Krüger, teNeues Verlag
Production by Alwine Krebber, teNeues Verlag
Color separation by Medien Team-Vreden, Germany

While we strive for utmost precision in every detail,
we cannot be held responsible for any inaccuracies,
neither for any subsequent loss or damage arising.

Bibliographic information published by Die Deutsche
Bibliothek. Die Deutsche Bibliothek lists this publication in the Deutsche Nationalbibliografie; detailed
bibliographic data is available in the Internet at
http://dnb.ddb.de

ISBN 3-8238-4552-7

Printed in Italy

Published by teNeues Publishing Group

teNeues Book Division
Kaistraße 18
40221 Düsseldorf
Germany
Phone: 00 49-(0) 2 11-99 45 97-0
Fax: 00 49-(0) 2 11-99 45 97-40
e-mail: books@teneues.de
Press department: arehn@teneues.de
Phone: 00 49-(0) 21 52-916-202

teNeues Publishing Company
16 West 22nd Street
New York, N.Y. 10010
USA
Phone: 001-212-627-9090
Fax: 001-212-627-9511

teNeues Publishing UK Ltd.
P.O. Box 402
West Byfleet
KT14 7ZF
Great Britain
Phone: 0044-1932-403509
Fax: 0044-1932-403514

teNeues France S.A.R.L.
4, rue de Valence
75005 Paris
France
Phone: 00 33-1 55 76 62 05
Fax: 00 33-1 55 76 64 19

www.teneues.com

teNeues Publishing Group
Kempen
Düsseldorf
London
Madrid
New York
Paris

teNeues